D0434174

THE GENDER AGENDA

Towards a Biblical Theology on Gender Identity, Reassignment and Confirmation

Steve Chalke

First published in Great Britain in 2018 by Oasis Books,
A brand of Oasis Charitable Trust.

Copyright © Steve Chalke, 2018

The right of Steve Chalke to be identified as the Author of the Work has been asserted by him in accordance with the Copyright, Designs and Patents Act 1988.

All rights reserved. No part of this publication may be reproduced, stored in a retrieval system, or transmitted, in any form or by any means without the prior written permission of the publisher, nor be otherwise circulated in any form of binding or cover other than that in which it is published without a similar condition being imposed on the subsequent purchaser.

Every attempt has been made by the Author to secure the appropriate permissions for material reproduced in this book. If there has been any oversight, we will be happy to rectify the situation and a written submission should be made to books@oasisuk.org

Scripture quotations are from New Revised Standard Version Bible: Anglicized Edition, copyright © 1989, 1995 National Council of the Churches of Christ in the United States of America. Used by permission. All rights reserved.

"In this welcome study, Steve Chalke regards gender identity not as a problem to be fixed or a norm to be upheld but as a mystery to be entered, with grace, understanding, and the expectation of being amazed.

Placing the contemporary church within the narrative of the Acts of the Apostles, Chalke invigorates this discussion by reminding Christians that we are the early church, and we all need to keep up with a God who is never calling us back to a static standard, but always ahead of us imploring us to catch up. Reading this short account is an exercise in rediscovering the diverse glory of God's kingdom."

Rev Dr Sam Wells, Vicar of St Martin-in-the-Fields, London

"'The Gender Agenda' forces us to take a deeper look at Scripture and understand that God's heart is radically inclusive. Like Steve, I believe we need a Revolution of Grace that ensures the whole Body of Christ can truly flourish."

Jayne Ozanne, Director of the Ozanne Foundation, founding member of the Archbishops' Council for the Church of England and member of General Synod

Steve Chalke is a social entrepreneur, justice campaigner, author, motivational speaker, Baptist minister and former UN Special Advisor on Human Trafficking. Having trained in theology, he founded the Oasis Trust in 1985, which he still leads today.

Oasis pioneers housing, education, healthcare, and many other community initiatives in the UK and elsewhere around the world. Steve also serves as the senior minister of Oasis Church, Waterloo, in central London.

Steve holds an MBE, a number of honorary fellowships and a doctorate from Staffordshire University, all awarded for his work in social inclusion and justice. He is also a Canon of Southwark Cathedral.

THE GENDER AGENDA

'Gender is between your ears and not between your legs' said Chaz Bono, the transgender writer, musician, actor and son of American entertainers Sonny and Cher.

If the last 50 years have witnessed fast changing attitudes around the issue of sexuality, now the debate is switching to that of gender, or to put it another way: from LG and B to LGBTQQIAAP.[1]

The issues surrounding gender dysphoria, reassignment and transitioning are undoubtedly complex, both medically and psychologically. But woven together with these concerns are a series of theological and pastoral questions which must be intertwined rather than held as separate conversations.

Although dismissed by some as 'a dangerous fad' and others as 'depraved', without doubt trans people are finding it a little easier than before to talk about their identity at school, at home and at work, despite the bullying and sometimes worse. [2] The discussion about gender-fluidity

[1] LGBTQQIAAP stands for Lesbian, Gay, Bisexual, Transgender, Queer, Questioning, Intersex, Asexual, Allies and Pansexual.

is on the rise and I believe that the Church has much to contribute that is distinctive, clear and central to this vital conversation.[3]

'Central to Christian theology is the truth that every single one of us is made in the image of God. Every one of us is loved unconditionally by God. We must avoid, at all costs, diminishing the dignity of any individual to a stereotype or a problem. Church of England schools offer a community where everyone is a person known and loved by God, supported to know their intrinsic value', wrote Justin Welby, the Archbishop of Canterbury, in the introduction to 'Valuing All God's Children: Guidance for Church of England schools on challenging homophobic, biphobic and transphobic bullying'.[4]

According to the Gender Identity Development Service (GIDS)[5], an NHS specialist service, offering support to children and young people who experience difficulties in the development of their gender identity: *'Topics related to gender identity – and issues that are relevant to many trans people's lives – have thankfully been receiving greater attention in the UK in recent years.'*

For most of us, our gender status (our biological sex) and our gender identity (the gender we identify with or feel ourselves to be as we develop) are one and the same. But, we are now waking up to the fact that this isn't

[2] The term 'transgender' only entered the Oxford Dictionary during the 1970s and 'gender non-binary' is no more than a few years old.

[3] Although more work needs to be done. According to a 2012 survey by the Equality and Human Rights Commission cited in CR181 'Good practice guidelines for the assessment and treatment of adults with gender dysphoria', Royal College of Psychiatrists, October 2013, about 1% of the UK population identity as transgender or gender variant in some way.

[4] Church of England: 'Valuing All God's Children: Guidance for Church of England schools on challenging homophobic, biphobic and transphobic bullying' Second Edition, Autumn 2017, https://www.churchofengland.org/media/4043522/ce-vagc-report-dl-v5-web.pdf

[5] The Gender Identity Development Service (GIDS) is a highly specialist clinic for young people presenting with difficulties with their gender identity. It is part of NHS England and was commissioned in 1989.

the case for everyone. A person, for instance, might have the anatomy of a woman but identify themself as a man, while others may not feel they are definitively either male or female.

Gender status had been traditionally assigned at birth on the basis of external genitalia. But, advances in developmental biology are teaching us that the reality is more complex; our gender identity is also shaped by sex chromosomes and sex hormones as well as internal reproductive structures.

The term 'trans' is commonly used as an umbrella and shorthand for anyone whose gender identity does not completely match the gender status (biological sex) they were assigned at birth. In the Health Service, the phrases 'gender non-binary' or 'gender non-conforming' are sometimes also used because of the growing understanding that sex and gender are different; that they are related in complicated ways, and that neither is a binary.

The mismatch of sex (as assigned at birth) and gender identity leads some to great distress and depression. Those affected feel trapped. They don't feel themselves in the body they are in. This has become known as gender dysphoria – now a recognised medical condition. As the NHS website puts it, *'Gender dysphoria is a condition where a person experiences discomfort or distress because there's a mismatch between their biological sex and gender identity.'*

Some people who have a strong and persistent desire to live according to their gender identity, rather than their biological sex, seek to transition; to undergo gender reassignment surgery and/or medical treatment which, in the UK, is now available through the NHS.

But, let's not go a paragraph further without stopping to acknowledge two important nuances:

First, the question of gender identity is far broader than the specific issue of gender reassignment. Gender reassignment is not the aim of every transgender person as they explore their gender identity. For some, although their assigned gender status at birth does not fully align with their gender identity (how they feel internally, their deepest sense of who they are) they do not feel the need or necessity to change their formal gender status.

Secondly, not all trans people are comfortable with the term 'gender reassignment'. Some choose, instead, to talk about 'gender confirmation'. Their point is that, far from having their gender changed or reassigned, what happens through the transition process is simply that their true gender identity (which because of the shortcomings of society's understanding of biology was wrongly called at birth) is finally recognised and confirmed.

LET'S TALK

There are some within the Church who loudly proclaim their opposition to the 'sin' of transgender expression, let alone of transition, whilst other more nuanced responses, which begin with tones of pastoral concern, only later reveal that they too are playing the same 'traditional' binary tune. The subtle shift from viewing transgender people as 'depraved sinners' to 'unfortunate victims of psychological pressures and mental illness' camouflages the fact that, in the end, as numbers of trans people have learned to their cost, the environment it creates is just as toxic for them. But the tragedy of this is a two-way thing. As Beth Malena writes, '*If the Church learns to see transgender Christians as perpetually disabled and in need of their benevolence, they risk forgetting that they are siblings in Christ, valuable community members, with gifts and knowledge to contribute.'* [6]

Much of the problem is exactly that: when we remove personal relationships with real people from the transgender debate, all we are left with is dehumanised stereotypes, caricatures and labels. And, in that context, just like any other phobia (an extreme or irrational fear of, or aversion to, something), transphobia soon breeds; non-understanding mutates into dislike, distaste, revulsion and eventually sometimes even hatred. This creates, as I see it, a series of negative outcomes:

---

[6] http://www.evangelicalsforsocialaction.org/resources/book-reviews/understanding-gender-dysphoria-by-mark-a-yarhouse/

First and foremost, for transgender people who too often find themselves on the receiving end of abusive comments and behaviours that these attitudes incite. Transphobic bullying (behaviour or language which makes a trans person feel unwelcome or marginalised because of their gender identity, whether actual or perceived, or because of a person's association with others who are, or are perceived to be, transgender) can have devastating effects on personal wellbeing, identity-formation and self-esteem, especially of the young. According to Nigel Genders, the Church of England's Chief Education Officer,[7] this is exactly why they issued their 2017 guidance for schools. *"We are equipping schools with support to ensure that they can create welcoming communities where human identity in all its forms is celebrated...One in ten pupils who are transgender have received death threats. Can you imagine how that can impact on a young life? More frequent is marginalizing through social exclusion, cyberbullying, verbal and physical abuse".* [8] Whenever these stigmatising and isolating attitudes are allowed to go unchallenged, school becomes scary and non-attendance more common.

Second, for the biblical writers and compilers who, I believe, are betrayed by such simplistic, over-literalistic but also, as I hope to demonstrate, selective readings of their sacred work.

Third, for our churches who, in our increasingly gender-fluid culture, are left having nothing more to offer than the supposed 'biblical' absolutes of binary gender stereotypes, and therefore little to bring to trans people who, like all of us, are searching for spiritual hope and direction.

As I've read various theological books and articles around transgender and gender dysphoria issues, I've become aware of a serious problem.

[7] There are approximately 4,700 Church of England schools serving one million children. Of these schools, over 750 are academies, making the Church of England the largest provider of academies nationally.

[8] Nigel Genders: "Why our guidance on combating bullying is part of our vision for education": 13 November 2017 https://www.churchofengland.org/more/media-centre/comment-and-features/why-our-guidance-combating-bullying-part-our-vision

Although exegesis should be, at core, about allowing the original biblical texts to speak to us rather than importing our pre-established views back into them, as we all recognise, each of us also brings our bias to any passage we explore. To suggest otherwise is to be disingenuous. Each of us comes to this issue, like any other, with a set of default assumptions. It is our duty, however, to do our best firstly to identify them and then to ask ourselves some serious questions about them as we proceed.

We all recognise that there have been loud voices within the Church who have opposed – on what have been, in their view, 'biblical grounds' – many of what are today accepted as fundamental rights; from the freedom, enfranchisement and finally the recognition of the equality of black and coloured people, to the establishment of the same equalities for women. Indeed, there are significant parts of the Church who still, on their particular reading and interpretation of the Bible[9], speak of the doctrine of the 'complementarity' of men and women rather that their 'equality', all of which acts as a thinly veiled disguise for the view that women are not qualified, because of their gender, to lead or teach in a church community.[10]

A view that is also often expressed is that, because gender transition is only possible as a result of modern medicine, it is interfering dangerously with nature, and therefore God's purpose and plan for us as a human race.

[9] Often a large part of the problem is that these churches proclaim loudly that they do not water down the Bible by interpreting it, but rather are 'Bible believing' and teach it straight. In truth, of course, it is always those who claim to have no bias of whom we should be most wary.

[10] Indeed, in his book 'Understanding Gender Dysphoria', IVP, 2015, Mark Yarhouse's theological anthropology depends on this concept of gender complementarity, although even he eventually concludes that the 'experience of true gender dysphoria....is not chosen' (p.81). Today, however, large numbers of theologians dispute that gender complementarity is the primary priority or category of the Genesis creation accounts. See 'Bible, Gender, Sexuality: Reframing the Church's Debate on Same-Sex Relationships', James V. Brownson, Eerdmans 2013, which presents an alternative interpretation of Genesis 1-2 that sits in line with much rabbinic understanding around these Hebrew texts.

If this is the case, however, perhaps we should ask ourselves similar questions around the advent of antibiotics, blood transfusions, heart surgery and IVF – all of which, when first developed, came with huge inbuilt risks and to this day continue to create societal and moral complications with which we wrestle.

What is often not considered is how we measure the impact of the taboo within huge parts of the Church which surrounds even the conversation about gender variation, let alone the non-availability of gender reassignment treatments on those who were, in the past, forced to live their whole lives feeling deeply uncomfortable with who they were?

What about those who just couldn't fit in, those who were written off as 'odd' or 'outsiders', who endured bullying, misunderstanding, loneliness and rejection? What about those who suffered throughout their lives from low self-worth or esteem, who couldn't even express what they felt because it was too 'shameful' or 'dangerous' to do so, or even because they didn't have the language to articulate their feelings?

What about those who still struggle today with anxiety, stress or depression? What about those who suffer from the curse of self-harm or who are even pushed to take their own lives, without ever feeling able to explain to anybody why? As one trans woman explained to me *"I cannot tell you how hard I tried to fight the truth about who I was, in order to be 'normal'; to fit into society, but the result was decades of deep depression and near suicidal unhappiness."*

In my view, the reason why trans people are becoming ever more visible is that social media has gone a long way to democratising our society and has given ordinary people the permission – and opportunity – to talk openly about who they are to one another for the first time. Far from fearing this conversation, I believe that humanity has much to gain.

None of this is to deny that there are still questions – both medical and psychological – that surround gender dysphoria and the safety of gender reassignment. For instance, we have a responsibility to engage with, rather than ignore or ridicule, the concern that some vulnerable young people might feel forced down a particular route and pushed into making what, with hindsight, might turn out to be a huge mistake? We do well to remember that 16 year old boys are as self-conscious of their body image as 16 year old girls, and that perhaps living in an over-sexualised society where there is so much pressure around shape and size, gender transition could become – for some – an ill-advised escape. Or, might a young gay person reach, misguidedly, the conclusion that they are of the opposite gender when they are not? Could gender confusion lead to misdiagnosis and a lifetime of regret and pain?

Our responsibility, therefore, is to create a safe space for young people to self-explore, without any pressure to reach premature conclusions. Equally, if a child is telling us that they are unhappy with their identity, it is our responsibility to listen rather than to ignore or dismiss them. The Church of England's intervention in November 2017[11], around the education policy for their schools, suggested exactly this approach. What the report does not go on to say is that it must be the duty of every responsible and compassionate society to accept the freedom of mature, self-understanding, gender variant people to determine their own future.

This is exactly why the Church needs to play its role in the conversation.[12] Let's not miss this important pastoral moment, nor the opportunity to empower transgender Christians to contribute their own voices, recognising that they may become our teachers[13], providing us with crucial

---

[11] Church of England: 'Valuing All God's Children: Guidance for Church of England schools on challenging homophobic, biphobic and transphobic bullying' Second Edition, Autumn 2017 https://www.churchofengland.org/media/4043522/ce-vagc-report-dl-v5-web.pdf

[12] Our prayer must be for the Church to engage without falling into the trap of maligning, misrepresenting or demonising those who bring other voices and opinions to the table. Instead, our task is to engage in a gracious discussion that refuses to write one another off as we seek a deeper understanding of these complex questions.

[13] See Austen Hartke's "Transgender and Christian" video series at

insights about what it means to be made in the image of God who, of course, transcends gender. Ideally, any discussion about transgender theology will be shaped significantly by transgender voices, whose first-person, self-disclosing and autobiographical reflections will deepen and enrich the conversation. We have a duty to include and to listen; indeed, not to do so will prove as vacuous and futile an exercise as was the discussion of black theology in a previous age without listening to or respecting the voices of black people.[14]

Mercia McMahon puts it this way, *"Theologians should be encouraged to write trans positive theology, and to maintain contact with members of trans communities who are also members of faith communities. As more trans writers of trans theology become established, those outsider perspectives would take on a different function: acting as a critique of debates that have become too insular. Nonetheless, the driving force of trans theology should transfer to members of the community once there are sufficient trans identified trans theologians to sustain the sub-discipline."* [15]

So why do I write? Because all this is a work in progress. Because I am a pastor who leads a diverse church in metropolitan London. Because I am the founder and leader of a large housing, education, health care and community development charity with many thousands of staff and beneficiaries. Because I know transgender people. Because I listen to transgender people. Because I have good friends who are trans people;

---

www.austenhartke.com/transgender-and-christian/ and Lisa Salazar's autobiography, 'Transparently: Behind the Scenes of a Good Life'.

[14] In 2016 the Corrymeela Community, which is based in Ireland, released an order of service for Trans Day of Remembrance. Written by a trans member of their community, the order of service is available at https://www.corrymeela.org/cmsfiles/blogs/Pádraig/20161120-TDOR-Liturgy.pdf

[15] Mercia McMahon in 'This is My Body: Hearing the Theology of Transgender Christians', edited by Christina Beardsley and Michelle O'Brien, Darton Longman & Todd, 2016. 'This is My Body: Hearing the Theology of Transgender Christians' includes contributions from many people associated with Sibyls, a UK-based confidential spirituality group for transgender people and their allies.

friends whom I respect; friends whom I love, friends whose pain and exclusion I have witnessed and wept over.

One of those friends wrote to me like this: *"Being transgender is not a choice...I had to do it...Pretending you are someone or putting on a mask just will not work and might in the end destroy you. You have to be yourself... Making the decision to transition was the best decision I have ever made. I feel better inside. I am more confident, more happy and I now actually like myself."*

THE REVOLUTION BEGINS

So where do we, as the Church, begin in all this? I believe that the key is to explore a theology of transgender inclusion and flourishing. And this, I suggest, should start with the ground-breaking story from the Acts of the Apostles of Philip and the Ethiopian Eunuch (Acts 8:26-39, NRSV); a controversial statement that serves as a precursor of all that was to come.

The recording, by the writer of Acts, of the meeting of Philip and the Ethiopian Eunuch is pivotal to the narrative of the early Church's understanding of the radical teaching of Christ in terms of how his Jerusalem-based followers begin to think about the implications of his message and take their very first steps into the wider world:

> [26] *Then an angel of the Lord said to Philip, 'Get up and go towards the south to the road that goes down from Jerusalem to Gaza.' (This is a wilderness road.)* [27] *So he got up and went. Now there was an Ethiopian eunuch, a court official of the Candace, queen of the Ethiopians, in charge of her entire treasury. He had come to Jerusalem to worship* [28] *and was returning home; seated in his chariot, he was reading the prophet Isaiah.* [29] *Then the Spirit said to Philip, 'Go over to this chariot and join it.'* [30] *So Philip ran up to it and heard him reading the prophet Isaiah. He asked, 'Do you understand*

what you are reading?' [31] He replied, 'How can I, unless someone guides me?' And he invited Philip to get in and sit beside him...

[36] As they were going along the road, they came to some water; and the eunuch said, 'Look, here is water! What is to prevent me from being baptized?' [38] He commanded the chariot to stop, and both of them, Philip and the eunuch, went down into the water, and Philip baptized him. [39] When they came up out of the water, the Spirit of the Lord snatched Philip away; the eunuch saw him no more, and went on his way rejoicing.

The impact and implications of this short but explosive story are multi-layered and far-reaching. It is fundamental both to the developing story of the early Church and therefore equally to the Church in the 21st century.

Good exegesis, as I suggested earlier, always attempts to begin with the text and its meaning to its original audience. Why was it written? How was it understood? What was its impact on the culture into which it was addressed? Only then can we ask the secondary questions around what it means for us today.

Commentators generally agree that the combination of the term 'eunuch' taken together with the title 'official' most probably indicates that this Ethiopian man was a literal eunuch as the result of having his testicles removed.[16] In Jewish eyes this puts him on the excluded list for more than one reason.

That the official is Ethiopian is scandalous. Judaism – of which the proto-church was still very much part – was for Jewish people. The followers of Jesus, the Jewish Messiah, believed and behaved as though the good news was Jewish good news for Jewish people or for those 'God-

[16] Non-literal uses of the term "eunuch" in New Testament passages include Matthew 19: 12 where Jesus explains, "For there are eunuchs who were born that way, and there are eunuchs who have been made eunuchs by others—and there are those who choose to live like eunuchs for the sake of the kingdom of heaven."

fearers' who would submit themselves to the lengthy process of proselytisation (including circumcision) before acceptance into membership. But, Luke does not identify the Ethiopian either as a proselyte, or a God-fearer. Instead, he presents him simply as one who is enquiring and questioning. From its outset, the Book of Acts sets out to challenge this assumption (albeit with the hindsight gathered from the fact that the author is writing after all the paradigm-shifting events he records have made their mark on the Church's thinking).

That the official is a eunuch is shocking. Even if this man's non-Jewishness had not been recognised, his gender status would have placed him totally beyond the pale on its own, whatever other steps he might take to make himself acceptable. As the restriction of Deuteronomy 23:1 reads; *'No man whose sex organs have been crushed or cut can join in worship with the Lord's people.'*[17]

It is therefore of dramatic significance that Philip commits to the radical course of action of baptising this Ethiopian eunuch. What is it that enables him to make this decision, with no reference to anyone else; long before Saul, who will become the great apostle to the gentiles, has even set foot on the Damascus Road; before Peter had met Cornelius the Roman centurion and baptised him and his family; or, most significantly, before the Council of Jerusalem was even a suggestion in the mind of James, the leader of the Jerusalem church?

I recognise that there is a tension here. For the record, I am not suggesting that a 1st century eunuch is the exact equivalent of a 21st century trans or intersex person. In my experience, some trans people find it a helpful analogy, whilst others don't see it that way because the story doesn't really go to the question of gender identity as such. It is, however, an extraordinary example of the early Church's understanding of the principle of radical inclusion as central to their mission and purpose.

---

[17] Deuteronomy 23:1

The point is this. Before the theological questions have even been surfaced – let alone been debated and resolved – Philip goes out on a limb. Why? Finding himself in this unprecedented situation, he can only be guided by his understanding of the teaching and example of Jesus – through the inspiration of the Holy Spirit – as he understands it and as the text makes plain.

But even so, why does the writer of Acts choose not only to include the story but to place it in such a prominent position in his narrative? If Philip was deemed by others to have made an error of judgement, to have rushed in inappropriately, to have overstepped his authority or position or to have acted out of line with the wisdom of the Church, then surely this embarrassing episode would have been erased from the record and therefore from history.

The fact that this scandalous story is preserved for later audiences – such as ours – and inserted at such an early stage in the Acts narrative, can be for no other reason than the early Church came to believe that Philip's actions, however shocking they appeared to be, were in line with the teaching and example of Christ, were inspired and guided by the Spirt of God and set the tone for their future mission.

Now we come to perhaps the most extraordinary dimension of this story. What is really going on here is no less than Philip's conversion. In the face of his encounter with this Ethiopian Eunuch – this sexual/physical/masculine 'other' – Philip is the one who has to make a huge choice. What does he really believe? Will he stick with the 'orthodoxy' of the text from Leviticus (and the prohibition it levies against eunuchs) or will he trust his instinct that through Jesus, whom he has dared to believe is the Messiah, the prophecy of the well-known text from Isaiah 56 (NRSV) (that of radical inclusion) is, at last, being fulfilled?

> [4] *For thus says the Lord:*
> *To the eunuchs who keep my sabbaths,*
> *who choose the things that please me*

and hold fast my covenant,
5 *I will give, in my house and within my walls,*
a monument and a name
better than sons and daughters;
I will give them an everlasting name
that shall not be cut off.

To state this principle another way: the Church has much to learn from those it considers to be outsiders. It is through opening ourselves up to those on the margins – through engaging with them, taking time to listen to their voices and stories – that we discover more of who we are.

---

[18] From the perspective of 1st century Jews or Romans (following the view of the Greeks), Ethiopians lived literally at the southern edge of the earth (see Homer *Odyssey* 1.23). This reference is exactly in line with the literary framework of the book of Acts. In Acts 1:8 Jesus' tells his followers, "But you will receive power when the Holy Spirit comes on you; and you will be my witnesses in Jerusalem, and in all Judea and Samaria, and to the ends of the earth." The text of Acts then follows this formula; first Jerusalem (Act 6:8-8:3). Then, Judea and Samaria (Acts 8:4-25 - Samaria was an area north of Jerusalem and the Samaritans, who we are told first received the gospel through the teaching of Philip and others, were the people who lived there. They were half-Jews and half-Gentiles). And, then the ends of the earth (Acts 8:26-40).

Regarding the Samaritans; following the acrimonious split between Israel's Northern tribes (which retained the name Israel) and the Southern tribes (Judea) after Solomon's death – the northerners built a new capital city which they named Samaria. But, when Assyria captured the northern kingdom in 721 B.C., though some were taken in captivity, many others left behind. At this point, the king of Assyria sent people from Cutha, Ava, Hamath, and Sepharvaim to live in the area. These foreigners intermarried with the Israelite population that was still there. The whole country became known as Samaria and its people as Samaritans – who were neither fully Hebrews nor fully Gentiles. The Samaritans built a temple for themselves on Mount Gerizim, which they believed was designated by Moses as the place where the nation should worship. They also had their own unique copy of the first five books of the Hebrew Bible (the Torah). As is well known, at the time of Jesus the Jews and the Samaritans still had a deep hatred of one another. Jesus, however, demonstrated a different attitude and inclusive approach to them.

So it is that the first fully Gentile convert to Christianity is not only a dark-skinned African but also from a sexual/gender minority.[18] The call to 21st century Christians could not be clearer; it is a call to be radically inclusive and welcoming – and, in line with the bold decision of Philip, to find the confidence to act in this way before all the questions have been surfaced, let alone answered; before the i's have been dotted and the t's have been crossed.

BACK TO BASICS

Inclusion is a major, though often ignored or even denied, biblical category. The word itself might never be used, but the theme of radical inclusion is embedded in Hebrew thought and within the biblical record from Genesis onwards. And it is this same, extraordinary but central, principle – celebrated and expounded through the life, teaching and example of Jesus – that guides the evangelist Philip when it is only his intuition he has to rely on. Jesus, as Philip knew, had the habit, not only of being seen with, but also of welcoming and befriending, all the 'wrong' kinds of people – from the perspective of the religious leaders and biblical experts of his day – as well as of saving up his damning disapproval for those who chose to use their religious authority to exclude others.

So it is that the story of the Ethiopian eunuch graphically demonstrates Philip's understanding of this core principle; the inclusiveness of Jesus' message. But it is more than that. From that moment on, although there would be (and to this day there continue to be) many struggles along the way – because attitudes, hearts and minds are slow to change – there is no room for issues such as those of race, sexuality or gender to place a person beyond the good news of the Kingdom of God.

In my view, this is where any Christ-centred theology of the Church's relationship to, and inclusion of, transgender people must begin. But, for those who would still want to insist that I have misrepresented a more complex question that is really about creation ordinances, what it is to be made in the image of God and the binary nature of that status as 'male and female', it is worth taking a closer look at the Genesis 1 creation text.

Firstly, we must ask, what does it actually mean to be made in the image of God? God, of course, is spirit. God has no physical body parts. And the scriptures are insistent; they describe God as both male and female rather than either/or. Whatever the phrase 'Imago Dei' implies (and there is much written about its implications), it is not about hormones and chromosomes, or the binary nature of humanity.[19]

Equally, although Genesis 1 speaks of the stark contrasts of the binary nature of God's creation: 'man and woman', 'earth and sea', 'day and night' or 'plants and animals', he (or to be more faithful to the biblical texts he/she) also creates the beautiful 'half-ways' of lakes and rivers, and dawns and dusks. Or, what of the ambiguities of Sea Anemones, which look like exotic underwater plants but have long been classified genetically as part animal and part plant?

Or, what do we make of the female Asian Sheepshead Wrasse fish – made famous by David Attenborough's Blue Planet II television series – which sometimes switches gender permanently from female to male, while other Asian Sheepshead Wrasse remain female for their whole lives? Gender transition is clearly not a 'western fad'. And, what of babies who are born intersex – people whose genitalia, chromosomes or hormones do not fit the typical definitions for male or female bodies? Are they not in God's image? To suggest any less is a crime against all scripture. God affirms the original goodness of all humanity.

To acknowledge that to be male or female is the norm, does not imply that to be intersex or trans is somehow inferior, or that it conveys some in-built form of censure or judgement. The *'norm'* does not equate to *'ideal'*, but simply to *'most common'*. The *'norm'* of having 'brown', 'black' or

---

[19] Imago Dei is a well-known and oft used term in theological circles meaning the image of God.

'blond' hair does not imply that being 'ginger' is somehow a sinful subversion, a disorder, or less than God's best!

We also know that although our dominant worldview and culture divides people into the binary categories of male and female and then describes them in terms of masculinity and femininity, this is not universally the case. For instance, there are a number of contemporary cultures that exhibit a greater gender diversity and where sex and gender are not divided along the neat lines – male and female, homosexual and heterosexual – with which we are so familiar.[20] Among some North American native communities, for example, gender has long been seen more in terms of a continuum than the traditional binary classifications we would recognise.[21]

These considerations are, in my view, why we should have reservations about the use of the term gender dysphoria, which can, for some, infer that we are talking about something that is wrong and needs fixing – or, more precisely, someone who is wrong and needs fixing. To speak instead of gender fluidity opens up a different kind of thinking and conversation; one which centres instead around individuals being given the space to grow more fully into who they are.

Back to the story of the early Church as depicted in the book of Acts.

A couple of chapters after the story of Philip and the eunuch, Acts goes on to record, in much greater depth, a similar incident in which Peter meets with, and subsequently baptises, the Roman Centurion Cornelius and

[20] This was, of course, also true historically; e.g. the fluid sexuality that both Greek and Roman societies were famous for and which forms the cultural background for the Pauline comments about sex and sexuality, especially in Romans, 1 Corinthians and 1 Timothy. For more, see my publication 'A Matter of Integrity' (2013) available from The Oasis Foundation at https://oasis.foundation/matterofintegrity

[21] For more information visit the World Health Organisation website at http://www.who.int/genomics/gender/en/index1.html

his family in Caesarea (Acts 10:1 – 11:18). But, it then informs us that, when Peter eventually returns to Jerusalem from his time with Cornelius, he finds himself plunged into the centre of a huge controversy and the object of severe criticism from the church there. The Jewish Christians still want to guard tightly the very boundaries which he has just chosen to ignore. It will take a long time for the penny to finally drop.

Contained in this exchange is a great insight into human nature and a repeated behaviour of the Church. Peter's negative experience at their hands has been repeated over and over again throughout subsequent centuries. Rather than being recognised and celebrated for the application of a Christ-centred approach to a new situation, instead the pioneer has too often been confronted with suspicion or even rejection. As David Smith puts it so poignantly, in his book *Mission After Christendom, 'Those who have broken new ground for the sake of Christ have found themselves carpeted by the guardians of orthodox faith'.*[22]

However, Smith goes on to suggest that: *'The very survival of Christianity ... depends upon the emergence of men and women able to think new thoughts and devise new strategies at the real frontiers of mission today.'* He adds the warning that such people are *'always likely to face misunderstanding, criticism and serious opposition. Like Peter the Apostle...those who are ready to confront the challenge posed by Western culture must not be surprised if they are accused of unorthodoxy, even heresy, or are verbally attacked by people who interpret their ... vision as something liable to undermine the moral purity and integrity of the Church of Jesus Christ.'*

Acts is the story of the journey of the early Church from its life as a localised, Jewish messianic sect to that of a worldwide [23], counter-cultural,

---

[22] David Smith, Mission After Christendom, Darton, Longman and Todd, 2003

[23] 'Worldwide' rather than 'Global'. Although the phrase 'to the ends of the earth' and the concept of Ethiopia being at the 'end of the earth (see footnote 18) was embedded into the popular speech and thought of the day rather than our modern term 'global', it is also true that by the 1st century AD this concept was beginning to be challenged and the idea that the earth must be a globe was slowly finding

subversive movement for reconciliation and radical inclusion which understands that Christ is saviour and Lord of all. Or, to express this same truth as a more universally applicable principle: the Spirit is moving on and the Church often finds itself either struggling to keep up or sometimes standing in the way of that progress altogether. Faithfulness, it turns out, is not the same as tradition. Following Christ is not always the same thing as 'doing what has always been done' – in fact, it is sometimes the opposite!

The local church that I lead, Oasis Church Waterloo in London, has five core values. We call them our Five 'I's – Intimacy, Involvement, Influence, Interdependence and Inclusion. Over the years I have had cause to learn that it is the last one, just as for that original church in the Acts account, which creates the most controversy for us.

I remember some years ago, a visitor, who, after I had preached on this very issue and our articulation of it as – '*we believe that we are made in the image of God, who loves every human being without exception. Our goal is to build an inclusive community that reflects this in our welcome and celebration of all people, whatever our background, social standing, gender, ability, sexuality or ethnicity*' – strode towards me at the end of the service. As we talked, or to put it more accurately, as I listened, he was clear with me: '*What you are doing is a disgrace – the Church is called to uphold godly standards*'.

I've had the chance to reflect on our visitor's words many times over the intervening years, and have concluded that, paradoxically, in one sense he was right. The Church is 'called to uphold godly standards'. However, the deeper question is this. Which standards are God's standards? Perhaps our biggest mistake is that we have been dogmatic about that which we should have been agnostic, and agnostic about that which we should have been far more dogmatic?

I am convinced that the standard we are called to advocate beyond all others is that of grace; of God's radical inclusion as most clearly

---

acceptance.

demonstrated through Christ. Put simply, our task is to be the indisputable proof that God is love – and that, to the extent in which we fail, we model, quite literally, 'dis-grace'.

Printed in Great Britain
by Amazon